# Close And Personal

Madeline Sharples

ISBN: 978-93-6354-299-0

First Edition: 2024
Rs. 200/-

***Cyberwit.net***
HIG 45 Kaushambi Kunj, Kalindipuram
Allahabad - 211011 (U.P.) India
http://www.cyberwit.net
Tel: +(91) 9415091004
E-mail: info@cyberwit.net



Printed at Repro India Limited.

# Contents

# Sad Memories

# Looking for A Prompt

I'm sitting here
sighing, shrugging my shoulders,
looking around the room
all while wondering
what words I'll put
on this page today. Usually
it's no problem, the words come
fast and furiously, but today
not so much. I hope that
is not a sign of bad writing times
to come. The dreaded
writers block
coming to haunt me
where it's never come before.
No that can't happen.
I know how to rev up
my poetry chops. The April
Poem A Day challenge
is on its way. I'll have more prompts
than I can handle
waiting to be written about
very soon.

# Eighty-year-Old Decisions

I think about it all the time as
I turn eighty this month
and should I continue my life as is:
exercising daily, eating healthy,
writing and reading away most of my days.
They say people over sixty-five
are at higher risk to get COVID-19.
But what about me?
Even though my health is excellent
wouldn't I be a higher risk than them?
Shouldn't I slow it all down
and spend most of my days
going forward laying snuggly
in my bed and just waiting patiently
with my head on my pillow
to die?

# Too Tired To Write

Before I even begin to write
my eyes start to close.
That's how tired I am.
I was up a lot of last night
worrying about Bob,
afraid his stomach issues
were the beginning
of something bad.
But no. he feels good today.
No more stomach problems
so, lost sleep over nothing.
Well when I did sleep
I had some interesting dreams:
one about a long-time friend
whom I called
a real piece of work.
Well, yes, he truly is.
And though he
might have taken offense
in real life
he just laughed it off
in my dream.

# Little Ben

I still love the memory
of my little boy Ben
and the many times
he'd stop his play, run to me,
grab hold of my leg and suck his thumb
just for a moment. He must
have been two or three at the time,
but no matter. He was there with me
giving me a wonderful gift.
Today he turned fifty.
He's a tall guy with dark wavy hair,
a beautiful smile, and he's
probably the nicest guy
I've ever known.

# The Spot Police

It all started with my dad.
He'd warn me at the dinner table,
pointing and wagging his index finger,
not to get a spot on my dress.
After all it costs money
to send it to the cleaners.
For the rest of my life
I've been spot phobic
like right now. I'm crazed
about the two tiny orange spots
on my kitchen counter.
I've used every product imaginable
to get them out,
and at this point the spots have faded
but not enough to totally disappear
from my view. And if I can see them
I have to keep working
to eliminate the tinges of orange
and turn them back
to their original pure white.
Any suggestions anyone?
I need that one magic bullet
so I can rest.
No thanks to you, Dad.

# The Saddest Day

This day, September 23,
is the saddest day
of the entire year.
It is the day, my son Paul
decided to end his life.
Even today, twenty-four years later
I stood at his grave
begging him to come back -
the only thing he could do
to make my life whole again.
But if he didn't care then,
why would he care
how I feel now?
People ask how I am
knowing the importance
of this day, and I always lie.
Oh, I'm fine, I say.
I could never explain
to anyone, how I feel today,
How I've felt on all the other
September 23rds
since he left me forever.

# Alex Trebek

My television friend,
Alex Trebek, died today
at age eighty
after a siege
of pancreatic cancer.
I had a date with him
every weekday
as I watched him host
Jeopardy, the only game show
I ever cared to see.
I loved his wit, his charisma,
his bright jabs, and
his bravery to do
his job in spite
of his cancer pain.
He had to wear a toupee
when his hair fell out
after his chemotherapy
and sit in a chair
to work. But nonetheless
he still had his same wonderfulness
up until the very end.

# Step Mania

I'm a step freak.
I've been counting then
since 2013 on my Fitbit.
Now I'm even worse.
Counting steps and
walking keep me focused
and grounded while
I stay home alone
during my husband's illness.
Steps take me out of myself
and my constant worries
about him.
They shut out my fears
that he's dying.
They cover up
the imaginings I have
that I'll never
see him again.

# Frankfurt Friends

I just spoke to Daniel
my Frankfurt Germany friend
who calls me almost every day.
We met Daniel and his wife
on a cruise and fell in love
all four of us. We visited them
and they came here - our families
came along.
Now we talk about this and that
probably his attempt to take
my mind off my loss.
It works a little
when we discuss COVID or what movies
we each saw the day before.
But today it got close to home.
I told him how empty it feels
here in this home where
I lived with Bob since 1979.
Well, his advice to me
was not to make any decisions
about staying or moving yet.
He's right of course.
I don't think my mind
is in the right place
to make any decisions
however big or small at all.

# My Favorite Car

I let go of another love today,
my cherry red Mercedes
that I've driven for sixteen years.
Ben put it on the market
for sixty-two hundred
and I clinched the deal
for six thousand even.
I was attracted to that car
right away. It had heated seats
and a weight heavy enough
to always make me feel safe.
And that same adoration
never changed in all these years.
The nice man who bought it
couldn't believe I really
wanted to sell. I have to,
I said. I don't need two cars.
I've decided to keep Bob's,
it's only two years old
with up-to-date electronics.
I can probably drive it
for the rest of my life.

# It's A Long List

Two miscarriages
Two C-sections
Webbed fingers
Bipolar disorder
Suicide
Cracked head in Morocco
Broken foot
Atrial fibulation
Pseudo gout
Rheumatoid arthritis
Skinned arm
Ruptured tendons
Difficulty walking
Diminished comprehension
Trouble speaking
Constant sleeping
No more bathroom control
No more eating
Severe sepsis
Death
Financial and house concerns
House sale
First move
In forty-two years

# Mother's Day Alone

This is my first Mother's Day
without Bob.
So that means
I got to spend two hours
with Ben and Marissa
visiting, questioning
and eating breakfast
until he had to leave for work.
After they walked out the door
I'm left alone
to read, to nap, to walk,
to cry and feel sorry
for myself
for the rest of the day.

# The Harpsichord Soundboard

Years ago a college-age man
asked me to decorate his
harpsichord soundboard
with flower paintings:
a pegasus, an artichoke,
and the parsley, sage,
rosemary and thyme herbs
circling the center.
I talked for almost an hour
to that man today,
now almost sixty-eight years old,
and he told me his best news.
He found his Hungarian
ancestors after falling out
with his adoptive family.
What a blessing
that I found him again.
He still has that harpsichord
And still cherishes
my paintings.

# Going Home

I went home this morning.
I drove to Manhattan Beach
parked by the library
and took my ever familiar
walk to the beach and
on the Strand. I could have
stayed for hours, this day
is so beautiful. But
twelve thousand steps
was my limit.
Then I ate my favorite breakfast
at my favorite breakfast place:
avocado toast at
Le Pain Quotidien. That really
made my day and made me
happier than I've been
for weeks. I'm going
to do that again
and again and again.
There is nothing to keep
me locked up here.

# I'll Miss Lee

My long-time friend Lee
died this morning
at three twenty-nine exactly
after a long bout with diabetes
and extreme anemia.
A hospice team came in
to take care of him
this past week, and lovingly
guided him to his final rest.
But I'll always remember Lee
as a long tall skinny guy
whom I worked with
on our high school newspaper.
He was quietly brilliant
and a wonderfully funny writer.
I was never sexually
attracted to him, but he
knew how to attract.
He was married seven times.

# The Brothers-in Law

I'm looking at a photo
of Bob and my brother
that I've put on
my computer desktop.
They have huge smiles
on their faces
as if they've been laughing
and are holding
each other tight around.
I wish I could
hold them tightly now
and revel in
their beautiful happiness
and friendship.
Instead I mourn them
and miss them
and will never ever
stop loving them.

# Haikus

An old friend and I
talked nonstop early this day
sharing everything

The hovering clouds
protect me from the sun's rays
during summer's heat

Walking was too hard
as the sun beat down on me
and dampened my clothes

Sit, breathe in and out
and maybe your heart will slow
to allow your work

A friend died in June
of ALS the worst death
We hailed her today

The little boy smiles
from his seat in his stroller
as I walk by him

I could only trudge
along my familiar path
My body felt stiff

I took a short cut
and now I have to pay up
and walk more later.

A few butterflies
flew by my side this morning
their wings like Monarchs

My left arm is sore
from the shingles vaccine shot
I want to lie down

# My Surroundings

## Darkening the Sky

Weather fights with weather
on this strange day.
The fog darkens the sky
and curls my hair
and then silently leaves
as the sun literally bursts out
spreading its pointed rays.
Then the fog takes over again
giving my arms a chill.
The cool air has won again.

# Climate Change

I was thinking climate change
as I walked this morning.
I started out at seven
with a temp of sixty-six degrees
and by the time I got home
at eight-thirty it was
already eighty-four.
This is June, known for its gloom,
somehow missing in action this year.
And for sure off the table
of government concerns.
Instead it's sweat time,
huffing and puffing time
as I crest the little hills
in my neighborhood.
I want my old June back.
It's so much more comfortable
to walk when it's cool.
It's time to discuss climate change again
and really make some headway.

# Dangerous Air Quality

I can almost see a blue sky
with a few clouds in it now
after days of gray ash
and dangerous air quality
in our midst.
Today the air quality
is moderate, a low seventy-five
not the dangerous levels
in the low one hundreds
a week ago. The fires are still
smoldering, destroying homes
and even little towns.
And the ash from these burning
buildings and forests
and people's precious things
has crept its way across the ocean
to England and Europe.
We here in southern California
are not the only ones
with congested chests and burning eyes.

## Needing A Jacket

There was a real Fall chill
in the air this morning.
It was so cool
I put on a jacket
for my walk.
Still the sun shined
through the gray clouds
contaminated by ashes
from our never-ending fires.
This life-threatening air quality
burns my eyes
and makes my nose run.
Still I venture out every morning,
wearing a mask, of course.

# My Surroundings

Last night I woke four times
every couple of hours
after vivid dreams
that disappeared from my mind
as soon as I opened my eyes.
I cannot get a good night's sleep
I cannot rest easily
I cannot warm up enough
to stop shaking.
What I need is someone
to hold me while I sleep
so I feel safe and free from the chill
of my life.
And I don't think
that holding warmth
will come any time soon.

# On Schedule

I'm still living
by watching the clock
having a set wakeup time
walking a certain number
of minutes a day
setting aside time
for writing, eating, reading
watching television.
In my life, I've always worked
on a schedule and now
even after Bob's death
and in the midst
of the pandemic,
when I don't need
to be anywhere at any time
I'm still acting like a person
on the run
and needing to always
be attuned to the hours
in the day.

# Eating Habits

I'm eating well
and enough. I do
the three meals a day thing
but mostly I eat
the same things over and over:
a high protein bar and yogurt
with fruit in the morning
unless I swerve over to
my used-to-be favorite
peanut butter on bread
or an apple.
For lunch I usually eat
a Trader Joes' ready made
salad. I like the one with
chicken, cranberries, slaw
and kale. I usually buy three
of those plus a couple
of outliers for the week.
But then I can't resist
the chicken salad Gelson's makes
so, I switch over to that as well.
Dinner is another story.
It's usually already cooked:
grilled salmon with asparagus
and a Thai pasta salad,
or I eat a chicken thigh
with the same sides,
or something from the freezer.
I've just discovered 130 calories

Lean Cuisine bowls and really
those aren't too bad.
They are just enough for me.
That's it. Week in, week out.
At least it helps
keep my weight steady
between ninety-five and ninety-six.
I'm not falling away
to nothing anymore.

# Lunch with Friends

Lunch in the garden
was the perfect thing
to do today.
The sky was pure blue
such when two wide-winged
birds flew overhead
they looked like paintings
on a blue canvas.
Little flowerpots rimmed
the grass where we were sitting
and giant trees were like statues
surrounding us.
I was sitting with two
writing group friends
eating the lunches
we each brought
having a conversation about
books, movies, gray hair, dogs,
and, of course, our health —
whether good or bad.
But then the small world shares
were the best of all.

# Empty and Lonely Days

The days get lonelier
and emptier.
I can't stand it.
I want the
front door to open
and welcome
people coming inside.
I want the table
set for at least twelve
and the burners
and ovens in the kitchen
full of foods I've spent
all day preparing.
Now the phone
hardly rings
the door stays shut
and the worst thing
of all
my bed is empty
on the other side.
There is no more
cuddling or holding
in my life
at all.

# Feeling Like A Slave

I feel abandoned
put upon
left to do
all the work.
Arrange for repairs
take care of the garden
sign the listing papers
and make sure
everything is perfect
before a buyer
comes by.
Then I'm the one
left to decide
on an offer
if one ever comes through.
Next I must take care of
all the work
of the move:
the throwing away,
the giving away,
the taking away,
Handling all the things
we lovingly bought together
and put into this home,
and touching each
one by one while deciding
what to do with it.
I resent it
I want him by my side.

After he died
I had to take care
of the finances
pay the bills
do the taxes
manage the money.
This other stuff
the selling, the moving
are way worse.
I must make the decisions
and I don't want
to make them
all by myself.

# Moving Grief

Today I was reminded of grief
while writing this afternoon
with my group.
I shared my thoughts
of moving from this house
with both good and bad memories
and going to a new place
with no memories at all.
That's what I want.
But I ask myself
will that help me move on
start my life all anew
or will it cause me to long
for all the forty-two years
that I lived here
with him and our boys.
Paul is gone; Bob is gone
only Ben remains, but he
is not here anymore except
for brief visits.
So I have nothing to leave behind
except for the memories
and the grief
and the many meals I served
on our dining room table
that seats twelve.

# More Work

I'm complaining to myself again
that I'm stuck doing
all the work. This morning
it was the trash.
That was Bob's job. He took
the trash out for all the years
until he became ill. His only
request was I refill the cans upstairs
with new plastic liners.
Though he sometimes forgot
to take out the food trash -
I keep it in the freezer.
He did that weekly job without complaint.
He owned it. And now
I own it and don't want to.
I don't want any of his old jobs
around the house. I want him here
to do them all himself
and give me a break
at least once in a while.

# Throwing Stuff Away

I began throwing away
old magazines in my closet
not looked at for years
notes from people
I've already forgotten
photos of folks
I want to forget.
I even found a letter
from my ex-husband
I've decided not
to look at yet.
But best of all
I found two short love notes
from Bob
No way will
I throw those away.

# Adrienne Rich

I am driven like Adrienne Rich
to write these short poems
every single day.
Her written words came
before her marriage.
No, I'm not that driven,
I'm not recognized
as she was though
I consider my words okay.
She was one of the first
confessional writers
and I followed in her path.
How else could I
have told my stories
about Paul, Ben, and Bob
and the smothering pain
always in my heart.
I've signed all the escrow paperwork
so it's almost a done deal.
Except and this is
a big except
I still don't know if
I'll end up with
enough money to move
to my new place.
That's what keeps me
up at night. Not that
I miss Bob beside me
or any other man

for that matter.
I worry about money
and that Bob left
our financial lives
in a huge mess.
At least he's gone
and doesn't have
to think about it anymore.
He left it all to me
all the signing
all the moving
all the worrying.
Maybe I can
find a way
to be gone too.

# Ruthless

I was ruthless today.
First I threw away
some stuff from
the big puffy envelope
Holly gave me after
Paul died. I had it
on the top shelf
of my office closet
never thinking
I could ever part with
one thing in it.
I got it down
a couple of days ago
let it sit on the floor
near my desk
until today. I packed
the few cassettes that
were in there, threw out
all the negatives
and one not-so-good painting,
signed Ian. The rest
I stuffed in a small folder
and stapled it shut.
Afterward, I took down
a box in the garage
that contained my years
and years of paper calendars.
I literally opened the box
took out handfuls

of calendars and dumped
them in the trash bin.
But when I got to the bottom
and found a couple
of notebooks, journals
I had written while
we were on Kwajalein.
I stopped throwing away.
I brought those journals inside
and packed them
with the other things
I'm taking with me
when I move.
Maybe I'm not
so ruthless after all.

# Watching Television

It's like clockwork.
I turn on the television
at six o'clock
and don't turn it off
until ten.
I watch news – usually
the Rachel Maddow show,
some food TV. I especially like
Chopped and Beating Bobby Flay,
And then I take the
little Apple clicker and
find a movie to watch
on Netflix, Prime, or HBOMax.
Lately I've been watching crap.
Stupid love stories with
young actors I've never heard of.
Last night was an exception.
Diane Keaton played a widow
In Hampstead. An unlikely romance
happens where no one
would have expected.
Then I'm off to bed
to read my latest book
for a few minutes.

# Neat Freak

I'm in a clean-up mode,
whole heartedly playing out
my obsession to keep everything
neat, in place, and in order.
My friend Eleanor says
that keeps me in control
because the recent events
in my life were so
out of my control.
Does that make me
feel any better? No,
I don't think so.
I'd rather have a messy house
with Bob living in it.
I didn't care about clean
when he was there.
He made messes all the time.
Compulsion didn't play a role then.

# Learning to Relax

I feel like
I've been running
in circles. I need
to stop, sit, lean back,
relax and let
my heart stop
beating so fast.
The beating has
taken over my body.
My teeth are clenched
my fingertips are cold
and I can't seem
to think anymore.
I'm holding my fingers
above the keyboard
trying to find out
the right keys
to put them.

## Faking Being Okay

One of my favorite quotes:
"People don't fake depression
They fake being okay,"
comes from Robin Williams.
He knew, he followed it,
and when he could fake
being okay no longer,
he killed himself.
That's me. You should
have seen me last night
in the lobby with Ben
waiting for our dinner.
I was smiling and hugging
and introducing Ben
to some new friends here
as if nothing was wrong,
as if I had nothing
bothering me at all.
And right now, I feel
like the lowest
of the low and there
is no way up.
But I'm good
at faking it. Maybe
faking will eventually
turn into a reality
and my life will be okay.

# Watching the Dogs

I've begun to notice
more than the
foliage and birds
and office buildings
as I take my daily
big long walk.
Ever since I fell
from being tripped
by a dog on a leach
I watch out for
those little critters
like a hawk.
I also see where
they leave their
yellow urine deposits
along the way.
The sidewalks are
tinged in yellow,
the street lamp posts
are bright yellow
at their base
from all the peeing
those dogs do.
Even the trees
have not escaped
the remnants of
the dogs passing by.
No wonder I've never
wanted a dog
in my life.

# Future Dreams

# Driving to Stay Awake

As I drive along La Cienega
on my way home
amidst the other cars and trucks
and SUVs and roaring sports showoffs
I find my head bobbing
my eyes wanting to close so badly
I almost lose control.
The sun is beginning to set
as its round shining ball
almost blinds me
over to the left.
While I maneuver myself
and my car in the right direction
the trouble is the lights.
They turn red every block or two
and waiting for what seems
like eons for them to turn green
makes me almost nod off
over and over again.
Even the last few miles
on the freeway and then
almost home on the neighborhood street
I keep thinking of going up the stairs
and laying down on my couch
until it's time to get up
to write this poem.

# Growing Hair

How did I know
that the collagen
I've been taking
to help grow my balding
head of hair would
also help grow
hair on my face.
It looked like I was
growing a beard
my sideburns were
so thick and dark.
But I showed them
But I went to see my brow
waxing lady who laughed
when I told her my sad
hair growth story
and got them
waxed off.
I also plan to continue
with collagen but just
two times a week
instead of seven.
It's good for keeping
my joints lubricated.
There's lots to be said
about that.

# Problem Feet

My feet hurt
I have huge callouses
on the outside
of each of my big toes
and another callous
in between my fourth and fifth
toes of my left foot.
I think it's from
my new walking shoes
I think they are too narrow
not that I've never had
these callouses before.
But now they are worse
and they hurt all the time.
That's not like before.
So this morning
I put corn pads on them
and so far so good
for my big toes.
Not so much for the
the other one.
It still hurts like hell.

# My Husband Is Dead

I don't know how
I am managing
to walk, to live in this house
to even breathe.
My husband of over fifty years
died last night.
He just stopped breathing
and thinking
and talking
and eating and walking.
He just stopped all the things
that one does to live.
He was done with all that.
He left me alone
to learn to walk again
without him. And I wonder
if I'll ever be able
to do that unless he's
by my side.

## Day Two

Practically all alone
thinking about
how I can go on
without him and learn
to handle all the things
he contributed to our lives.
I read emails and texts
from people sympathizing
and saying they are sorry
and want to help
any way they can.
They express love for him
and complement our long lives
together. If only they knew
really knew the pain in my heart
in my head, in every shaking
finger such that
my whole body
shivers so that
I don’t think I can
bear this pain much longer.

# Just Enough

It's like the floodgates have opened.
He's not here
but his and our friends
have come en masse
at least virtually.
Or they have called,
texted, emailed,
and sent bouquets
of white roses and orchids
and lilies.
I don't want any of that.
I almost cringe
when I see more flowers
on the doorstep
What do I need them for?
I remember after Paul died
my first clean up job
was throwing out
the dead flowers.
I couldn't stand the smell.
These new flowers
will end up in the can as well.
I can't remember ever
feeling this bad and inadequate.
Here I am a widow for less than
Two weeks and nothing
makes sense to me.
And they keep coming at me
asking questions about our will

our living trust
our social security accounts
our mortgage. Why the hell do I
have to know all this,
less than two weeks since
my husband died. Less than
two weeks since he left me
with all these things I have to do
to get my life back into order,
so that I can go on living without him
which to be truthful
I don't want to do.
I want to go too.
I'm eighty. And that for sure
is just enough.

# Tired and Cold

I don't want to do anything.
I'm cold, I'm always
so, so tired
and I just want
to crawl right back in bed.
And of course
there are things to do:
the thank you notes
paying a few bills
telling people my husband died
sending out death certificates.
No wonder I don't
want to do anything.
Those chores are terrible.
Those chores should
never have to be done.
Those chores make
me want to cry.

# No Concentration

I watch a movie
most every night
I listen to a podcast
while I walk in the morning
and if anyone asks me
what I saw,
what I heard,
I couldn't tell them.
I don't listen and see anymore
I can't concentrate
I can't keep my brain focused.
I said to myself this morning
when a discussion was announced.
Good, now if I listen carefully
I'll know what that's about
and almost immediately
my mind turned to other things
while the discussion was going on.

# How I'm Doing

I'm a mess
I keep making mistakes.
I don't have my act together
so that I feel foolish
and embarrassed
about the things I'm doing.
And now I wonder
if I'm getting demented.
I'm old enough
for that to happen.
But I'd rather be
well than sick
in any way.
When I go
I just want to drop dead
and be thought of
as one smart old lady.
But that won't happen
the way I'm behaving now.
I better think carefully
before I do anything
at all.

## What I'm Doing

I always can find
something to do.
Take my big long walk
when I first wake up
eat some breakfast -
usually a protein bar
or a slice of bread
with peanut butter on it
and then look through the folders
I have to deal with that day
or the next.
Later I'll either lie down
on the coach, my go-to nap place,
read a book or sleep
until it's time to take
another walk before sunset
and before the news comes on.
I try to wait before having
my first glass of wine,
that usually leads
to a second and a third
while I eat some dinner
and find a movie to watch
until I call it a day.

# How I Do It

I don't know
how you do it,
she said when I told her
I'm writing a poem
and a journal entry
every day. Even through
his long illness
and now in the three weeks
since he died.
I have to, I said.
It's how I do grief.
I need to put my pain
on the page. I need
to let the grief
come out by tapping
on my computer.
It's like a grief exercise
and when I'm finished
I can breathe a bit easier
and rest for a while.
I fell asleep
in his yellow leather chair
this afternoon.
It was as if I belonged
in there. It was as if
I were sitting
on his lap
The chair is
in the family room

close by to my place
on the couch.
And night after night
we'd sit there
in our places
watching television
sharing a bottle of wine
discussing the daily politics
before dinner
and then afterwards.
Now I have both places
all to myself.
More than I need
Much more than I want.

## Like My Mother

I'm already acting
like my mother.
From the day her husband
died at age seventy-two
when she was sixty-eight
she said she wanted to die
and made all her children's
and friends and family's
lives miserable.
She became a miserable old lady
and she didn't care whom
she offended.
She didn't even stop
that kind of talk
when our son took his life.
She said she wanted
to drown herself
in the ocean like Virginia Woolf
And be done with it.
I told her to stop
that kind of talk,
but she never did. Except
when she was dying.
Only then did she ask for help.
Unfortunately for her,
it was much too late.
As for me, I don't want
to be late for my destiny.
and I won't tell anybody
about it either.

# Where Do I Go

More and more I think
I can't live like this anymore.
There is no place to go
no place to turn to
no one to sit down with
and just talk.
Losing my husband
during the Pandemic
has made mourning him
and finding a way
to get over his death
much much harder.
It has taken all I have
just to live through each day
to put one foot
in front of the other
and walk, eat, read,
write, watch television
and then go to bed.
The worse part
is that every day
is the same. Every day
I stay here feeling cold
I stay here and feel shaky,
I stay here and feel blue
all alone.

# Get Over It Already

My dear old friend
called this morning
practically yelling with the question
what's going on with you?
Not how are you getting on?
How are you feeling?
What are you doing
without Bob in your life anymore?
Does that mean I should
erase him and my feelings
for him already
and get on with the rest of my life?
Well, I don't think so.
I want to spend more time
wallowing, mourning
and thinking about him
Throughout these lonely days
I want to keep him
in my life for as long as I can
I'm the only one
who can do that now.
The others want me to be
over it and free.
No not yet.

## Reading About Grief

Lunch with friends cancelled
because of wind
so I start a new book
called Good Grief
about a thirty-three-year-old widow.
She can't visualize herself
as a widow. Widows are supposed
to be gray-haired old ladies like me.
Not young, a bit overweight
from eating too many waffles
and dressed in her husband's
old comfy shirts like her.
I don't visualize myself
as a widow either
or think about my husband
as dead and gone.
I still hear his noises
all over the house
I still visualize him sitting
In the yellow leather chair
in our family room.
And I still have his ashes
in our bedroom armoire.
Maybe I'll think
about him as dead
after I've spread
those waiting ashes
into the sea.

# We're Still We and Our

I find myself
talking about "we"
and "our" lately.
I can't let go
of him even
in small conversations.
He's always with me.
It's not that I care
about that.
It's not that
I ever want him
out of my life.
It's just that
I cannot move on
without him
If I continually think
of him as the other
part of me.
Well it's no wonder
we were together
for over fifty years.
How does one sever
a relationship like that?
How does one dump
the man who was
the love of my life?

# Diamonds Are Love

I wore the diamond necklace
Bob gave me last year
probably for the fifth time.
It is still beautiful
and fits around my neck
just perfectly.
When he died I thought
about selling it
but now I don't think so.
Once I get out into the world
again, I could wear it all the time
It's a simple, a strand of gold
with tiny diamonds sparkling
around it. I don't think
I need the money
so why not learn to enjoy it?
There will be loads
of other things to give away
or sell once I start the huge
breakup of this house.

# Lonely Or Depressed

What is the difference
between lonely and depressed?
Not much, I think.
The way I see it,
I sit and stare,
I hear noises and startle
I wait for a call
a hello, an invitation
for dinner, or lunch
or anything. But, no.
nothing happens
and I still have to go
to bed alone every night.
And every day
I eat alone too.
How could one
not be depressed
with loneliness like that?

# I'll Try

Okay, I'll try
I told my sister
I'll try to
participate more.
Call back the people
who reached out to me.
I know I'm friendly
when I see
someone I know
outside or in the hall
but nothing seems
to have resulted
from that.
Yet, today I got
a great invite
to join two women
at next week's
Wine Wednesday event.
Just up my alley.
Now those are the kind
of people I want to meet
not the little old ladies
who drink water
with ice and lemon
to accompany and augment
their dinners. Nah!

# I Am Blocked

I've been stalling
lollygagging over breakfast
reading the next
old The New Yorker
from my pile
reading the news
taking the trash out
filing away last month's
journal entries into
my secret folder.
Finally here I am
writing my daily
ten-minute poem
which stinks, by the way.
And is much too short
and void of meaning
or details. But still
I keep my fingers moving
the advice I got early on
when I didn't have
an idea in my head
to write about.

## Reading A Page Turner

I'm reading a page turner.
But I'm not sure
I'll finish by tomorrow's
book club meeting.
I read a bit, snooze a bit
that's no way
to finish a book.
I also find distractions
returning a package
having a cup of tea
at Starbuck's
fixing a spinach
and salmon salad
Taking my dinner order
to the dining room.
There is always something
to get in the way.
Even writing this poem
is a distraction.
okay, as soon as I
write down the last period
I'll get back to the book.

# No Curls for Me

I'm a hair failure.
I thought I could
dry it naturally
with some curling
potion infused in
and voila, I
would produce
a head of curly hair.
Well, to say it simply,
that didn't work at all.
What I'm left with is
a combination of
straight and waves
that go every which way
that looks, to put it mildly,
absolutely awful.

## Thankful

They keep saying
we have a lot to
be thankful for.
Yeah, Yeah, I say.
sure we do
or maybe only
they have a lot
to be thankful for.
I don't. Not after
living without Bob
now over a year
I'm not thankful
that he got
sick and died
last year.
I'd be thankful
if he hadn't.
I'd be thankful
if he were here
living with me
lying in my bed with me
eating dinner
with friends and
celebrating Thanksgiving,
walking with me every morning
sharing that bottle of wine
with me every night
and kissing me before
we settled in to sleep

on our respective sides
of the bed.
So no. You guys out there
have a lot to be thankful for.
I don't.

## Time to Change

I have to change my life.
I need to get busy and
start writing again. I cannot
keep lying down and hiding
myself in my afternoon
sleeps and drowning myself
in dreams. That's not getting
me anywhere anymore. And
it takes me away from where
I want to end up – a sequel to
Papa's Shoes, another poetry
chapbook and maybe just writing
to keep me sane and functional
again. I told someone today
I am a published author, and
right now I hardly believe it
myself. Tomorrow I will
begin my new regime.

www.ingramcontent.com/pod-product-compliance
Lightning Source LLC
LaVergne TN
LVHW091224150826
845673LV00003B/1005

* 9 7 8 9 3 6 3 5 4 2 9 9 0 *